Enriching Your Prayer Life
How to Study the Prayers of the Bible

Markus McDowell

An Imprint of Sulis International
Los Angeles | London

Published by Keledei Publications
An imprint of Sulis International
Los Angeles and London
www.sulisinternational.com

Copyright ©2018 by Markus McDowell
First Edition

All rights reserved. No part of this publication may be reproduced in any form by any means without permission from the publisher, except for the inclusion of brief quotations in a review.

Library of Congress Control Number: 2018907124
ISBN (print): 978-1-946849-30-4
ISBN (eBook): 978-1-946849-29-8
1. Religion 2. Christian Life 3. Prayer

All Scripture quotations, unless otherwise noted, are from the New Revised Standard Version of the Bible, copyrighted, 1989 by the Division of Christian Education of the National Council of the Churches of Christ in the United States of America, and are used by permission. All rights reserved.

Join the author's Readers Group
and receive a free book at
https://www.markusmcdowell.com/send-gift/

Table of Contents

Preface 1
Introduction 3
Types of Prayers 9
Prayers of Praise 13
Thanksgiving Prayers 19
Petitions and Intercessions 25
Prayers of Confession and Repentance 29
Prayers of Lament 35
Prayer-Vows 39
Blessings and Curses 43
Studying the Bible 49
A Three-Part Method for
Studying the New Testament 55
"Behind" the Text 61
"In" the Text 71
"In Front" of the Text 81
An Example: Studying the Prayers of the Bible......87
Resources 95
A Note from the Author 97
About the Author 98

Preface

This book is a companion book for my series of volumes entitled *Praying Through the Bible*. It can serve as an introduction, before reading any of the others, or as a way to add an in-depth background to the study of the prayers after reading one or more of the volumes. (For the current list of volumes available, visit https://prayingthruthebible.com or search Amazon.com or other online retailers for "McDowell Praying Through the Bible."

The goal of this book, as all the others in this series, is to help us enrich our own prayer through studying that rich variety found in the prayers of the Bible.

We'll begin with a description of the Praying Through the Bible project: how it began, how I approach the study of each prayer passage, and my view of the purpose and practice of prayer.

The next eight chapters focus on the nine types of prayer found in the Bible. We'll examine one prayer in terms of purpose, structure, content, prayer, along with some examples.

Since studying the prayers of the Bible involves Bible study, just like any other passage, the next five chapters focus on why we study the Bible and why we need to. These chapters will introduce the three-part method used in the Praying Through the Bible project, along with examples of how the technique works when applied to biblical prayers.

The final chapter before the conclusion is an example—we'll apply all of the preceding to the prayer found in the prayer of Naomi in Ruth 1.8–9.

The conclusion provides an overall summary and additional resources for the further study of the prayers in the Bible.

Thanks for being a part of this project!

Introduction

Those of us who pray sometimes feel that our practice of prayer could be better. We might wish we prayed more often, or that the words sounded better, or that our words was more genuine. Maybe we wonder if we are praying the "wrong" things—whatever that might mean. Most of us were never taught how to pray—we just mimicked what we heard.

After more than twenty-five years of studying prayer, I still cannot say that I understand prayer in all its richness and purpose. No one can, because prayer is, to a certain extent, a mystery. It is an ongoing conversation with the divine Creator of the Universe. But we *can* learn more about prayer and thereby grow in our practice.

Scripture is the best place to begin. Not only is it the authoritative word of God, but it also contains hundreds of prayers, teachings about prayer, and mentions of prayer. As I studied the prayers, I found a richness and variety that I had not seen before. I saw new possibilities for prayer in their content, structure, times offered, postures to accompany them, and types of prayers.

It occurred to me that, if I could study every mention of prayer in the Bible, not only would I learn a lot, but it would also enrich my own prayers. What better resource than God's Word?

I had been writing and speaking about prayer for many years before I began the project, and had many hundreds of people talk to me about prayer. They would often tell me that their prayers seemed rote, or that they didn't know what to pray, so they said the same things over and over again. Some said they pray because they think they should, but do not believe they are doing it "right." Others even told me that they had almost stopped praying because it seemed like a lifeless act. My heart went out to these people, because I had some of those same thoughts.

In 2011 I began working on a project I called "Praying Through the Bible." It began on a blog, with a short study and application about the first mention of prayer in the Bible.[1] During the next few years, I worked my way through each prayer in Genesis, then Exodus, and so on. The blog gained popularity and attracted followers all over the world. My own understanding of prayer grew through emails from my readers and comments on the blog.

---

[1] See "The Personal Name of God (Gen 4.26)," *Praying Through the Bible, Volume 1 (Genesis–Joshua)* (2015).

Introduction

The Rest of the Books on Prayer

Many asked me for a book of these studies—something they could use for personal and group study and devotion. I published the first volume, covering Genesis through Joshua, by expanding upon the blog posts and offering more detail and application, while still keeping each study short enough for a daily devotional or a class study. The book sold well, and the demand kept up, so I continued publishing volumes as I wrote enough for a book. As of this writing, there are three published volumes: Genesis through Joshua, Judges through Second Samuel, and First Kings through Second Chronicles. A fourth volume, Ezra through Esther, will be published at the end of 2018. In addition, at the request of many, I have released eBooks for each of the individual books, as well as beginning a podcast of many of the prayers for those who prefer to listen. (See the Conclusion for where you can find these resources.)

Each chapter in the books study one prayer passage or connected passages. Some are actual prayers—that is, they include the words of the prayer. Other chapters address passages that teach something about prayer; still others look at passages that only mention or refer to prayer, without including the words. Sometimes a prayer passage is only one verse or a part of a verse; sometimes it might cover many verses.

Each prayer study is divided into three parts: background, meaning, and application. These work together to make up a "devotional commentary," which means that its primary purpose is application through study and understanding. To meet that goal responsibly, we seek to understand each passage within the context of its section and book. Since the Bible was written in ancient times, we also look at the historical context when helpful. Likewise, we look at some cultural aspects that might affect an understanding of the passage. If relevant, we examine the original language used or a literary technique employed. Anything that helps us understand the prayer passage is fair game.

Once we have a sound understanding of the prayer in its contexts, we can explore how the writer might have meant it and how the original readers might have understood it. After we have investigated the background and meaning, we are ready to ask what we can learn from the prayer that will help us with our own.

The Practice of Prayer

We'll begin by describing. the nine types of prayers. We'll practice them each in the application sections of the later books, which can sometimes seem artificial: I'm only going to pray thanksgiving prayers today. But remember, all of this is a means to an end. As you work through this book and later volumes, and practice your prayers, remember that this unique activity of "talking with God" is primarily about relationship. It is not about praying a certain way or using certain words, phrases, or categories. One of my favorite stories that emphasizes this point is an old Jewish story.

Introduction

There was once an illiterate cowherd who did not know how to pray, so instead, he would say to God: "Master of the Universe, you know that if you had cows, and you gave them to me to look after, I would do it for nothing, even though I take wages from everyone else. I would do it for you for nothing because I love you." A certain sage chanced upon the cowherd and heard him praying in this manner. The sage said to him, "You fool, you must not pray like that." The cowherd asked him how he should pray, and the sage set about teaching him the order of the prayers as they are found in the prayer book. After the sage went away the cowherd soon forgot what he had been taught and so he did not pray at all. He was afraid to say the usual prayer about God's cows because the sage had told him it was wrong to say such things, on the other hand he could not say what the sage had told him because it was all jumbled up in his mind. That night the sage was reprimanded in a dream and told that unless the cowherd returned to his spontaneous prayer great harm would befall the sage, for he had stolen something very precious away from God. On awakening the sage hurried back to the cowherd and asked him what he was praying. The cowherd told him that he was not praying anything since he had forgotten the prayers the sage had taught him, and he had been forbidden to tell God how he

> *would look after his cows for nothing. The sage begged him to forget what he had told him and go back to his real prayers that he had said before ever he had met him.[2]*

Prayer is different for each of us, just like the communication between any two people is different. This book lays the groundwork for studying the prayers of the Bible, as a means to explore the prayers themselves, which in turn is intended to enrich our own prayers.

Each of us must find our own way, however. Not all of us are spiritual sages nor cowherds. My hope is that this book (and the other volumes) will serve as a guide and model for you to find your own way, so that for you, like the cowherd, God will find something precious in your prayer life—not because you followed a set practice in this book, but because you have found a way of prayer that helps you express your heart for God. Whatever you learn, make it yours, and then give it back to God as a gift. If that means telling God you will look after his cows for free, while you stand dirty and unkempt in a field, so be it.

---

[2] David G. Gross and Esther R. Gross, *Jewish Wisdom: A Treasury of Proverbs, Maxims, Aphorisms, Wise Sayings, and Memorable Quotations* by (Fawcett Books, 1993).

Types of Prayers

This chapter will describe the prayers found in the Bible in general terms, by categorizing them into nine types or categories.

By "type" I mean the content and the purpose of the prayer. Here are the nine:

1. Praise

2. Thanksgiving

3. Petitions

4. Intercessions

5. Prayers of Confession and Repentance

6. Laments

7. Prayer-Vows

8. Blessings

9. Curses

You may be familiar with all of these, most people know of some of them. But you might not be sure what they are. For example, what is the difference between a praise prayer and a thanksgiving prayer? Between a petition and an intercession? And does anyone really pray laments, prayer-vows, or curses any more?

In practice, there is some overlap between some of these, and all of them have connections with to one or more of the others. But it is helpful to think of them separately as we study them, so we can focus and learn about each type.

Some of the types will be found together in one prayer, but more often than not (and perhaps surprisingly) most prayers in the Bible are of one kind. Some occur more frequently than others. The Psalms contain every type—not surprising since the book of Psalms is a book of prayer-hymns.

Most of us tend to use only a few of these types, the most common being petition, intercession, and thanksgiving. Studying *all* of the types, and learning their purpose and how to use them, will help us have a more consistent, rich, engaging, and effective prayer life.

Each type has its unique value and purpose, so we will examine each one on its own. We should not forget, however, that these kinds of prayers are connected and can be combined. For example, in the book of Exodus, some types repeat in a precise pattern. Suffering (slavery) leads the Israelites to offer a *petition*; the petition leads to an answer from God (choosing Moses as a leader) but also brings further difficulties (the Egyptians make the Israelites suffer). The sufferings cause the Israelites to offer more *petitions*, *intercessions*, and *vows*, and that results in God delivering the Israelites. The deliverance leads the people to offer prayers of *praise* and *thanksgiving*.

As we study each prayer type, remember that the flow of the prayers is important, too. If we petition God for deliverance and then neglect to praise or thank Him, we have missed part of the rich connectedness of prayer types. God desires a relationship that does not place us in the role of a child who takes without thanks, nor that of a spouse who always cries out for help but never shows gratitude. It is a relationship that ebbs and flows, gives and takes, cries and comforts, declares and responds.

Prayers of Praise

A "prayer of praise" is a prayer that focuses on the character of God. It is not a prayer that thanks God for something, although thanksgiving prayers and prayers of praise are connected. But there is value in considering the two types as separate, even if they often overlap in practice. Consider this: while a thanksgiving prayer offers thanks to God for something He has done, a prayer of praise honors God because of who He is as Creator, the One who sustains us, and the One who loves us with perfection. Praise is about the recognition of God's being and character, rather than thanking Him for something he did.

Think of a famous person from history, someone you respect and admire above others. Let's leave Jesus out of this exercise—think of a typical human. Maybe it is a president, a king, a sports figure, a scientist, or an artist. You might, at first, be more in awe of who they are, rather than being thankful for something they did. The respect or reverence that you feel is because of their character and being—their legacy, so to speak. The awe you experience is similar to the reason for a prayer of praise.

It may be difficult for us to offer pure prayers of praise. Most of us are pretty good at thanksgiving—we receive something from someone, we thank the person. But the Bible contains plenty of models of praise-prayers for us to study and mimic. The opening chapters of Revelation provide a good example. Chapters 2 and 3 depict a pretty sad scene among the churches in Asia Minor. They are poor, they have forgotten their way, pagan culture has influenced them, or they are selfish. A faithful Christian might feel quite disheartened. Chapter 4 is a scene that takes place in heaven. God is on His throne, surrounded by twenty-four elders and all manner of creatures; all are praising God. In such a dismal state of affairs on earth and in the church, they praise God because they know that He is always on the throne, He is always in control, He is *always* sovereign. We offer prayers of praise to God because He is in His holy temple; because He has the Final Word. We offer prayers of praise because *we* know how this story ends, regardless of how bad everything might be now.

Some of the longest prayers in the Bible are praise of praise, or contain prayers of praise. A praise prayer is the subject of one of the oldest prayers in the Bible, the "Song of Victory" in Judges 5.2-31 (which also includes a blessing and a curse at the end.) Another powerful praise prayer is that of King Solomon at the dedication of the Temple in both 1 Kings 8.23-26 and 2 Chronicles 6.14-42.

Yet praise prayers can be short and simple, too:

> *"For he is good,*
> *for his steadfast love endures forever," (2 Chron 5.13; 7.3; 20.21; 29.30).*

Notice that this prayer does not thank God, but describes Him. Likewise, the prayer of Hannah, after God grants her a son, describes God, even though she was responding to God's answer to her petition. Here is the beginning of the prayer:

> *"My heart exults in the LORD;*
> *my strength is exalted in my God.*
> *My mouth derides my enemies,*
> *because I rejoice in my victory.*
> *There is no Holy One like the LORD,*
> *no one besides you;*
> *there is no Rock like our God. (1 Sam 1.26ff)*

Another example is a simple praise prayer (offered by a pagan king, no less!) He praises God as creator, and then praises him for the king in Israel:

> *Blessed be the LORD God of Israel, who made heaven and earth, who has given King David a wise son, endowed with discretion and understanding, who will build a temple for the LORD, and a royal palace for himself. (2 Chron 2.12)*

Sometimes a prayer begins with praise before moving on to confession or petition:

> *"O LORD God of heaven, the great and awesome God who keeps covenant and steadfast love with those who love him and keep his commandments; 6 let your ear be attentive and your eyes open to hear the prayer of your servant that I now pray before you day and night*

> *for your servants, the people of Israel, confessing the sins of the people of Israel, which we have sinned against you. Both I and my family have sinned. (Neh 1.5ff)*

In many passages, we are told that there were praises offered, even though the author did not include the words of the prayer. For example, 1 Chron 16.4:

> *He appointed certain Levites to serve before the Ark of the Lord, to celebrate, to give thanks, and to praise the Lord the God of Israel.*

When my children were young, we visited many of the ancient church cathedrals in Europe. My daughter, who was seven years old, did not like entering those massive edifices. My wife and I thought that it was because of the crypts and grave markers inside. My mother had recently died, so we assumed the reminders of death made her think of her beloved grandmother. Once, on a trip to France, we visited the famous cathedral in Strasbourg, and I decided to have a serious conversation with her about her fears. As we walked down the center aisle towards the massive transept, I held her hand and asked why she was so scared of cathedrals. She stopped and leaned into me, looked up with wide eyes and said, "Because they make me feel *so* small. It scares me. I feel *this* big—" and she held out a thumb and forefinger close together.

I knelt down and put my arm around her. "Yes, they *do* make us feel quite small, don't they?" I said. "But you know what? They built them that way *on pur-*

pose. They designed them to be so big, and to appear to almost reach up to heaven, to help us remember how powerful and *awe*-some *God* is. And yet, despite all that scary power, we can still come to Him, and be with Him, just like we can be in this cathedral: because He loves us."

A look of wonder came into her eyes and she cocked her head to the side. "Really?" From that moment, she enjoyed visiting cathedrals. She lit candles for her grandmother in their chapels and touched the foot of Saint Peter's statue in Rome. She came to understand that the feeling of *smallness* was appropriate before God, for it reminds us of His power and His love.

That is why we offer prayers of praise.

Thanksgiving Prayers

Thanksgiving prayers occur throughout Scripture. The word for "thanksgiving" appear 140 times in the Old Testament and 53 times in the New Testament. Moses, Joshua, the kings of Israel, and the prophets all offer thanksgivings. Often, a group of people assembled together offer them. Paul's letters are full of thanksgiving prayers. Jesus gives thanks for people, for the fact that God hears him, and before meals. In Revelation, elders, multitudes, and beasts offer thanksgiving to God twenty-four hours a day. In each of those instances, they thank God for something He has done for them—as an individual or as a group. Sometimes, though, thanksgivings are offered when we might not think that one makes sense. For example, the prophet Habakkuk stands on the walls of his city and sees disaster coming as an enemy bears down on Israel.

> *I hear, and I tremble within;*
> *my lips quiver at the sound.*
> *Rottenness enters into my bones,*
> *and my steps tremble beneath me.*
> *I wait quietly for the day of calamity*
> *to come upon the people who attack us.*
> *Though the fig tree does not blossom,*
> *and no fruit is on the vines;*
> *though the produce of the olive fails*
> *and the fields yield no food;*

> *though the flock is cut off from the fold*
> *and there is no herd in the stalls,*
> *yet I will rejoice in the LORD;*
> *I will exult in the God of my salvation.*

In spite of the coming disaster, he praises God for who He is, then he thanks him because He is the God of his salvation.

Sometimes, thanksgiving prayers are inappropriate. For example, Jesus tells a parable of a religious leader who goes up to the Temple to pray. He sees a tax collector—people who worked for the Roman oppressors and got rich off their own people—and he thanks God that he is not like him or other "undesirables." Jesus criticizes this sort of thanksgiving.

Thanksgivings are structured in many ways; they can be long or short, they can be spontaneous or well-planned. In these studies, we'll define a thanksgiving as a prayer which thanks God for something specific that He has done—usually for the one who is praying, or for his or her community. For example, after King Cyrus agreed to allow the Jews to return to Jerusalem and rebuild the Temple, Ezra and the others responded in this way:

> *...they sang responsively, praising and giving thanks to the LORD,*
> *"For he is good,*
> *for his steadfast love endures forever toward Israel." (Ezra 3.11)*

Or, in 2 Corinthian 1.11:

> *...as you also join in helping us by your prayers, so that many will give thanks on our behalf for the blessing granted us through the prayers of many.*

Thanksgivings are also given before meals, as Jesus did often (Matt 15.36, 26.27; Mark 8.6; 14.23; Luke 22.17, 19; John 6.11, 23). The church continued this tradition, especially during the Eucharist after their meals (Acts 27.25; 1 Cor 11.24).

As with all prayers, thanksgivings are relational. They are part of the give-and-take of an ongoing conversation with God. Just like human relationships, thanksgivings can include understanding and misunderstanding, dialogue and silence, joy and pain. Thankfulness is part of any genuine relationship, but it is not all of it. Thanksgiving prayers do not stand alone. They are connected with the prayers that came before: petition, vows, confession, repentance, and requests for forgiveness. In this case, a thanksgiving prayer is the response of gratitude. Still, we might offer a thanksgiving prayer merely *because* God allows us to have a relationship with Him, much like we might say "thanks for loving me" to a spouse or friend. It also means that we can offer a thanksgiving in the midst of struggles, like Habakkuk, just as we might say, "thank you for being here and comforting me" to a friend who visits us during a difficult time. Thanksgivings might be the most connected of all the prayer types because of the variety of situations in which it can be offered. While a petition, vow, or confession are usually offered on particular occasions, a thanksgiving prayer is always appropriate. This is why Paul tells the Thessalonian church to "give thanks in all circumstances; for this is the will of God in Christ Jesus for you" (1 These 5.18).

Paul almost always begins his letters with a thanksgiving—this was common in letter-writing in that world, to thank the gods for the recipients. But Paul often turns it into a prayer:

> *I give thanks to my God always for you because of the grace of God that has been given you in Christ Jesus (1 Cor 1.4)*
>
> *I do not cease to give thanks for you as I remember you in my prayers. (Eph 1.16)*
>
> *We also constantly give thanks to God for this, that when you received the word of God that you heard from us, you accepted it not as a human word but as what it really is, God's word, which is also at work in you believers. (1 These 2.13).*

Prayers of thanksgiving are often found connected with prayers of praise. For example, when the Temple was first built, there were a group of musicians committed to provide singing. We read that they used the lyre in "thanksgiving and praise to the Lord" (1 Chron 25.3). Similarly, when Hezekiah reinstituted proper worship, the Levites and priests were commissioned to "give thanks and praise" (2 Chron 31.2). An excellent example of the connection between the two is found in Revelation 11.17:

Thanksgiving Prayers

> *"We give you thanks, Lord God Almighty,*
> *who are and who were,*
> *for you have taken your great power*
> *and begun to reign.*

Thanksgiving prayers may be the form of prayer we are most familiar with after petitionary prayers. In them, we thank God for something he has done for us.

Petitions and Intercessions

Petitions and intercessions are both common in Scripture. Both ask God for something. A petition is a prayer that asks for something for the one who is praying. For example, "God, please help me be generous today." It might seem selfish to ask things for ourselves, yet it is part of a genuine relationship. Children ask their parents for things. It is a sign of reliance. Of course, over-reliance can become selfishness. Someone who is always asking for something does not experience the genuine richness of a true relationship. But petitions are an appropriate part of the give and take, and found often in scripture.

The first prayer mentioned in the Bible is a petition:

At that time people began to invoke the name of the LORD. (Gen 4.26)

Since the person offering a petition is praying for themselves, the subject is often personal: family, safety, or guidance:

And God heeded Leah, and she conceived and bore Jacob a fifth son. (Gen 30.17-22)

David inquired of the LORD, "Shall I go and attack these Philistines?" (1 Sam 23.2)

Fearing that we might run on the rocks, they let down four anchors from the stern and prayed for day to come. (Acts 27.29)

Jesus prayed a petition in his time of great anguish:

> *"My Father, if it is possible, let this cup pass from me; yet not what I want but what you want." (Matt 26.39)*

An intercession (or intercessory prayer) is one which asks for something for someone else. You might pray that a friend has successful heart surgery, or that a missionary group is safe and effective. Praying on behalf of someone reflects that, as believers, our relationships are both vertical and horizontal. We pray *to* God the Father as our sustainer and redeemer; we pray *for* someone else as a loved one, fellow believer, or fellow human.

The Israelites asked Samuel to pray for them:

> *"I will pray to the LORD for you."*
> *"Do not cease to cry out to the LORD our God for us, and pray that he may save us from the hand of the Philistines."*
> *Samuel cried out to the LORD for Israel, and the LORD answered him. (1 Sam 7.5-9)*

Sometimes an intercession is offered by a group, not just one person.

> *While Peter was kept in prison, the church prayed fervently to God for him. (Acts 12.5)*

Jesus offered many intercessory prayers—not surprising since he is often described as our intercessor:

> *...but I have prayed for you that your own faith may not fail; and you, when once you have turned back, strengthen your brothers." (Luke 22.32)*

Both types of prayers are frequent in scripture, though not as often as prayers of praise. We might find this surprising because most of us tend to ask for things more often than we offer praise, thanks, confession, or repentance. This may be why we are sometimes dissatisfied with our prayers: we are missing the richness of a genuine relationship because we focus on only one or two types of prayer.

Why does Scripture suggest that prayers of intercession and petition should not be the most common types offered? The answer, as noted above, is that we need a relationship with God. But there is more to it than that. God first desired a relationship *with us*. He created us, He continues to sustain us, and He makes it possible for us to know Him. If petition and intercession stand alone, we turn God into a divine Santa Claus or a personal counselor. Scripture does not portray God in such a way. Instead, He is described as a father, mother, savior, creator, king, nurturer, and sustainer. Petitions and intercessions are only *part* of an ongoing relationship. If we use them alone, they are an insult to God and the relationship. Imagine if your child, spouse, sibling, or friends never thanked you, praised you, or said they were sorry. What if they only asked you to give them things? It would not be much of a relationship..

Petitions and intercessions show our dependence on God and are appropriate within a full relationship. Because we praise, thanks, confess, and vow—we can also ask. In fact, we are encouraged to do so:

> *"Ask, and it will be given you; search, and you will find; knock, and the door will be opened for you." (Matt 7.7)*

Prayers of Confession and Repentance

Prayers of confession and repentance may be the most intimate form of communication. There would be no need for confession and repentance if we did not fail our created purpose and damage our relationships with God and others, resulting in the need to confess and repent.

Confession is not something we are prone to do. We do not want to confess our misdeeds; we want to explain them. We might say, "I was afraid" or "he provoked me beyond my limits." Those excuses might be true. But confession and repentance do not address the *reason* behind a sin; they speak to the *fact* of sin and the consequential damage.

Confession and repentance are about admitting our misdeeds and pledging to do better. "I am sorry I hurt you, and I promise I will never do/say that again." We often want to add "but…" to an apology. However, true confession rejects explanation or rationalization. If we try to offer defenses and reasons, we soil the process. Instead, confession should be a declaration and repentance a pledge to be better.

Confession and repentance are linked, but they are different. Confession is the first part: I declare my sin before God, my spouse, family, friends, and/or congregation. When we name the sin, it begins to lose its power over us. Turn on the light, and shadows become common and ordinary. "It is not a goblin's head; it is my basketball!" "It is not a gnarled old man with a knife; it is the way the shadow of a tree shines against the curtains!" When we move our sin from *inside* of us to *outside* of us, we begin to allow God to deal with it appropriately. Once you have told someone of your sin, it is more difficult to ignore or rationalize it. You are held accountable—and accountability is crucial for the connected prayer type of repentance.

Repentance is the next part. The word comes from an old Anglo-Norman/Old French word meaning "to renounce (something)," "to cease (to do something)," "to express contrition or regret." After confessing, we express our regret for the damage or hurt we have caused, and reject that behavior. A prayer of repentance disavows the act. "That is not who I am; it is not who I should be, and I reject it; I am now on a new path to avoid it in the future because I see it for what it is." A prayer of confession without repentance, or repentance without confession, would be incomplete.

The Bible is full of confessions and prayers of repentance. In much of the Old Testament, they are connected with sin sacrifices. Leviticus and Numbers both describe how they are to be offered to be cleansed of sin and forgiven. For example:

> *When you realize your guilt in any of these, you shall confess the sin that you have committed. (Lev 5.5, see also 16.21; 26.40; Num 5.7.)*

These actions of sacrifice emphasize that one must confess sins to be forgiven for them. Jesus emphasizes the same thing in the Lord's Prayer,

> *"And forgive us our debts,*
> *as we also have forgiven our*
> *debtors." (Matt 6.12)*

During the conquest of Canaan, when the people failed to follow God's commands, tragedy fell upon them. Joshua went to the leader of the rebellious group and told him he must confess to God.[3]

The New Testament continues the idea of the importance of prayers of confession and repentance:

> *If we confess our sins, he who is faithful and*
> *just will forgive us our sins and cleanse us from*
> *all unrighteousness. (1 John 1.9)*

James even suggests we should confess not only to God, but to each other:

> *Therefore confess your sins to one another, and*
> *pray for one another, so that you may be*
> *healed. (Jas 5.16)*

Sometimes leaders confess the sins of a group of people, even though it may be that the leader did not sin. Ezra confessed the sins of his people for not separating themselves from nonbelievers, as God had asked them

---

[3] Josh 7.19.

to do.[4] Nehemiah offers similar prayers for his people.[5] In Nehemiah 9.3, the people themselves confess their sins together as a group. Today, congregations and groups of believers rarely engage in public and group confession, despite the numerous examples in the Bible. This is probably a testament to the difficulty of admitting we are wrong. While some of us might confess in private, or (more rarely) in public, we do not often hear leaders take on the sin of their congregation or a group and confess on their behalf as their leader.

If you do not know how to pray a confession, the Psalms are a good resource. Often, the words can be recited with little or no change to fit your circumstances. For example, Psalm 38.18 is an excellent beginning for a prayer of confession:

> *I confess my iniquity;*
> *I am sorry for my sin.*

It is a simple declaration followed by a simple statement of repentance. Nehemiah offers another excellent example the book of his name, 1.5-11:

> *"I now pray before you day and night for your servants, the people of Israel, confessing the sins of the people of Israel, which we have sinned against you. Both I and my family have sinned. 7 We have offended you deeply, failing to keep the commandments, the statutes, and*

---

[4] Ezra 9-10.
[5] Neh 9-10.

the ordinances that you commanded your servant Moses."

A more complex prayer is David's prayer of confession after his affair with Bathsheba in Psalm 51.[6] The structure of the confession is a good template for our prayers:

1. Request for mercy (51.1–2)
2. Confession of the sin (51.3)
3. An acknowledgment that the sin hurts God and others and God would be justified in punishing (51.4–5)
4. An expression of knowledge that only God can forgive and cleanse (51.6–12)
5. A look to the future (repentance) (51.13–18)
6. A statement of knowledge that God wants sincere and humble followers (51.18–19).

When we sin, we can always be forgiven and start anew —otherwise, our sins would continue to build up, burying us under the weight of failure and guilt and separating us from God. This was the reason for daily, monthly, and yearly sacrifices described and commanded in the Old Testament. For Christians, there is no need to offer those oil, grain, or animal sacrifices, because of the sacrifice of His Son took the place of those sacrifices. That perfect sacrifice was more horrific than any

---

[6] Read the story in 2 Samuel 11-12.

animal sacrifice, but also more effective because it was God's sacrifice.[7] It need be done only once. Then, in confession and repentance, we take part in that sacrifice. Jesus becomes an offering for *our* sins of his own free will, and we are cleansed and forgiven.

In prayers of confession and repentance, we throw ourselves upon God's mercy, acknowledging that He is our only hope to begin again. We make a statement about our future, and we commit to being renewed, to live differently, and to serve Him. Such prayers offer us the opportunity to offer ourselves in humility and to be lifted up by the Judge himself, who says, "go, my child; you are no longer guilty. The cost of sin has been paid. You are a forgiven and innocent being—now go out and live like it."

---

[7] Some people are outraged that the Jewish religion slaughtered thousands of animals a year for their own sins, but often those same people are not outraged that a man was slaughtered for their sin. We should be shamed that it was necessary, and grateful that it was offered.

Prayers of Lament

A lament is a prayer that cries out to God in pain and loss. It does not ask God for anything (though a petition often follows a lament). Imagine a small child in pain and cannot fathom what is happening to them. The child cries to their parent because the parent is the caregiver, the authority, and the nurturer. The child may even wonder why the parent is allowing the pain, though the parent may be unable to stop it—an illness or a cut on the arm. In Genesis 21.16, a mother cries out because her son is about to die in the desert: "And as she sat opposite him, she lifted up her voice and wept."

A lament may be the most open of prayers, because they are an emotional cry. Sometimes a lament even questions God, or calls Him to account! In a time of seemingly meaningless suffering, a lament may come to the lips of a believer almost unbidden: "Why, God?!"

You may have heard that one should never question, criticize, or be angry at God. But laments often do exactly that, and so demonstrate the richness and relational nature of prayer. They are God's way of allowing us to be honest and open with Him and to express, with pure emotion, how we feel. After all, if a relationship forbids certain discussions, then it is a limited relationship. There is nothing improper about a lament, because one *still* turns to God, like a child crying out to a parent—even in anger or a feeling of betrayal. James commands his readers to offer laments: "Lament and mourn and weep" (Jas 4.9).

But laments, like all other prayers, do not stand alone. They often end with a petition, and sometimes even with a thanksgiving or praise prayer. While God does not always reveal the reason for suffering, those who pray laments in the Bible find comfort in His presence, even if relief does not come—just as a baby finds comfort in its mother's arms, even if the pain does not go away.

There are laments spread throughout the Old Testament. Hagar cries out when she and her son are banished to the desert to die.[8] Joshua and the leaders of Israel lament when they lose a devastating battle.[9] Laments are found most often in the Psalms and in the Prophets, especially those written during the time of Exile.[10] As you might guess, the book of Lamentations is one long prayer lament.

The New Testament is not without laments, either. One of the most famous is from Jesus, while on the cross, quoting a Psalm of lament (Ps 22):

My God, my God, why have you forsaken me?

---

[8] Gen 21.16. See "Hagar's Lament and Petition (Gen 21.16)" in *Praying Through the Bible, Volume 1 (Genesis–Joshua)* (2015).

[9] Joshua 7.7–9. See "A Lament (Joshua 7.7–9)" in *Praying Through the Bible, Volume 1 (Genesis–Joshua)* (2015).

[10] For example, see Psalms 17:13–14; 35:4–6, 26; 44; 58:7–10; 137 (more than 20% of the Psalms are laments). The entire book of Lamentations is a highly developed lament-prayer.

> *Why are you so far from helping me, from the words of my groaning?*
> *O my God, I cry by day, but you do not answer;*
> *and by night, but find no rest.*

Jesus uttered other laments as well over two cities and Jerusalem.[11]

The Psalms include both individual laments and community laments: a congregation or other group of believers can offer a lament in a time of tragedy, suffering, and loss.

A lament is a good example of the relational nature of prayer and is a type that can add some meaningful richness to our prayer life.

---

[11] Matthew 11:20–23 (cf. Luke 10:13ff); Matt 23:37–38 (Luke 13.34–35).

Prayer-Vows

Prayer-vows, like laments, are uncommon today, at least in the modern Western world. Yet they are prevalent in scripture. Perhaps this is a form of prayer we should revive to add richness to our prayers.

Vows offered to a deity were common in the ancient world among all people and religions. A prayer-vow is a conditional agreement with a god or goddess. The offerer promised to give a sacrifice or a gift, in return for the god or goddess doing something for them. For example, in 296 BC, the Roman consul Appius Claudius Caecus prayed that, if his patron goddess Bellona would grant him victory in battle, he would build a temple in her name.[12]

The Old and New Testament both contain similar prayer-vows. Sometimes the offerer promises something to God and asks nothing in return. For example, a Nazarite vow is one in which a person promises not to cut the hair, drink wine, or be around unclean things for thirty days.[13] John the Baptizer took this vow, as did Paul.[14] Samson is one of the most well-known examples of a man taking a Nazarite vow, though this

---

[12] Ovid, *Fasti*, vi.201–205. The Temple was built several years later in Rome, and dedicated on June 3, 296 BC.

[13] The full description and requirements of the vow is found in Number 6.1–21.

[14] Luke 1.15; Act 18.18, respectively.

vow was for his entire life rather than just thirty days. These one-sided vows which do not ask for anything are vows of dedication—dedicating oneself to God in some particular way for a time.

Acts mentions men who are under prayer-vows (one is Paul), though we are not told what the vows were. The context shows Paul's was probably a Nazirite vow); the others were likely the same:

> *...Paul said farewell to the believers and sailed for Syria, accompanied by Priscilla and Aquila. At Cenchreae he had his hair cut, for he was under a vow. (Acts 18.18)*
> *"So do what we tell you. We have four men who are under a vow." (Acts 21.2)*

The second type of vows are conditional agreements with God, and are common in the Bible, too. The offeror promises to give something to God, or His work in the world, if He grants their petition. For example, Hannah vows that if God allows her to give birth to a son, she will dedicate him to the service of God:

> *"O LORD of hosts,*
> *if only you will look on the misery of your servant,*
> *and remember me, and not forget your servant,*
> *but will give to your servant a male child,*
> *then I will set him before you as a Nazirite until the day of his death. He shall drink neither wine nor intoxicants,*

> *and no razor shall touch his head." (1 Sam 11-13)*

Jacob does the same, though his vow is more self-centered:

> *If God will be with me, and will keep me in this way that I go, and will give me bread to eat and clothing to wear, so that I come again to my father's house in peace, then the LORD shall be my God, and this stone, which I have set up for a pillar, shall be God's house; and of all that you give me I will surely give one tenth to you. (Gen 28.20-22)*

Since these vows are pledges to do something *if* God does something, we might wonder if they are self-serving. While a prayer-vow could be misused in that way, a genuine prayer-vow is part of the relationship between God and us. It is a give-and-take, a promise to each another, and a way of showing loyalty. We are not telling God that he *must* do something; just that if He does, we will thank Him by offering a special gift in place of a usual thanksgiving. It might be money, time, or some other benefit to God and His mission.

Two-sided vows are serious business. Psalm 66 cautions that, if you dare to offer such a vow, you had better keep it. One should think carefully and responsibly *before* offering a prayer-vow. Jephthah offered a rash one in Judges 11, with tragic results when he found out his vow meant he had to do something he had not foreseen:

> *And Jephthah made a vow to the LORD, and said, "If you will give the Ammonites into my hand, then whoever comes out of the doors of my house to meet me, when I return victorious from the Ammonites, shall be the LORD'S, to be offered up by me as a burnt offering."*

He probably thought it would be an animal that met him at his gate, but it was his daughter.[15] We should treat vows of this type with care.

The one-sided prayer-vow is an opportunity for us to show our dedication to God and a way for us to hold ourselves accountable to Him. We might vow to pray three times a day for the next month, or refrain from critical words for a day, or to skip lunch for a week and spend that time in study and prayer.

Prayer-vows may be the most neglected form of prayer for modern believers, but are important if we are to have a rich prayer practice. They help us to hold ourselves accountable to God or dedicate ourselves to Him.

---

[15] Some question whether he should have kept the vow, since it involved the sacrifice of his daughter; or whether this was an example of Israel's fall from God in offering human sacrifices. We will examine his vow in the next volume, "Rash Vows (Judg 11.30-31)." (There is a later writing that describes the daughter's long lament: Pseudo-Philo, *Liber Antiquitatem Biblicarum* 40.5–7. If you are interested in a technical discussion of the prayer, see my analysis in Markus McDowell, *Prayers of Jewish Women: Studies of Patterns of Prayer in the Second Temple Period*, 100–104.)

Blessings and Curses

Blessings and curses appear in Scripture as separate prayers, but usually appear together. The reason for this is that they are a particular kind of petition. They do not ask God for something as much as wish it or hope for it, usually in the presence of another person or in public.

A blessing asks that good will come upon someone, that they will receive a gift, or that God will bless them in some other way. Curses do the opposite: they ask that punishment or harm may come upon someone. In this way, they are petitions that God do something, though they often do not ask God directly for the blessing. For example, Naomi says to her daughter-in-law, "May you be blessed by the LORD, my daughter" (Ruth 3.10).[16] Noah says, "Cursed be Canaan, the lowest slaves shall he be to his brothers" (Gen 9.25).[17] There is an element of "hope" rather than a direct request.

I use the word "hope," yet prayer-blessings and prayer-curses are stronger than a mere "I hope this happens." In the ancient world, blessings and curses (especially the latter) were thought to have an almost magical power. If one said them correctly, in the right circumstances, they would happen. The understanding of curses and blessings in the Old and New Testament is

---

[16] See "A Blessing for a Saint (Ruth 3.10)" in *Praying Through the Bible (Vol 2): Judges-2 Samuel*, 2017.

[17] See "Noah's Blessings and Curses (Gen 9.25-27)" in *Praying Through the Bible, Volume 1 (Genesis–Joshua)* (2015).

rarely, if ever, presented in that "magical sense." Still, they have more power than just "I hope God brings justice upon you." Prayer-blessings and prayer-curses attest to a firm belief in the spoken word and the power of God.

Blessings in the Bible are pronounced upon individuals, groups, or nations. Leaders and priests utter them; ordinary people speak them. Blessings can be pronounced upon God (and often are):

> *"Worthy is the Lamb that was slaughtered*
> *to receive power and wealth and wisdom and might*
> *and honor and glory and blessing!" (Rev 5.12)*

In these, the blessing almost becomes a kind of praise-thanksgiving-blessing, that good should come to God because He deserves it.

Non-believers in the Bible sometimes offer blessings. Melchizedek blessed Abram (Gen 14.19-20):

> *"Blessed be Abram by the God Most High,*
> *The One who created the heavens and the earth.*
> *And blessed by the God Most High,*
> *Who delivered your enemies into your hand."*[18]

King Hiram blessed Solomon (1 Kings 5.7); the Queen of Sheba blessed the God of Israel (1 Kings 10.6).

---

[18] See "Melchizedek Blesses Abram (Gen 14.19-20) in *Praying Through the Bible, Volume 1 (Genesis–Joshua)* (2015).

Blessings can be for something specific or merely a general pronouncement of good. They can be formal or informal, spontaneous or traditional.

Jacob (Israel) blesses his grandsons in a traditional "deathbed" pronouncement upon children (Gen 48.15–20).[19] The priest Levi blessed all the people of Israel (Lev 9.22):

> *Aaron lifted his hands toward the people and blessed them...* [20]

Prayer-blessings fill the book of Ruth, and are pronounced upon a number of people.[21] In the New Testament, Elizabeth blesses Mary (Luke 1.42, 45); Jesus blesses children (Mark 10:16) [22] and offers blessings at meals (Luke 9.16). Paul's letters are filled with teachings about blessings, blessings on God, and blessings on his readers, sometimes for others:

> *Bless those who persecute you; bless and do not curse them. (Rom 12.14)*
> *Blessed be the God and Father of our Lord Jesus Christ, the Father of mercies and the God of all consolation... (2 Cor 1.3)* [23]

---

[19] See "Israel blesses the Sons of Joseph (Gen 48.15-16, 20)" in *Praying Through the Bible, Volume 1 (Genesis–Joshua)* (2015).

[20] See "Aaron Blessing the People (Lev 9.22) in *Praying Through the Bible, Volume 1 (Genesis–Joshua)* (2015).

[21] Ruth 2.4, 12, 19, 20; 3.10; 4.11-12, 14.

[22] See the parallels in Matt 19.15 and Luke 18.17.

[23] See also 1 Cor 7.40; Eph 1.3.

Curses, likewise, can be general or specific, formal or spontaneous. In scripture, they are often the result of some evil done by a person or a warning of what will come if someone does something forbidden. Joshua curses anyone who might try to rebuild Jericho (Josh 6.26):

> *Cursed before the LORD be anyone who tries*
> *   to build this city—this Jericho!*
> *   At the cost of his firstborn he shall lay its foundation,*
> *   and at the cost of his youngest he shall set up its gates!*[24]

Jeremiah curses the day of his birth and the person who announced it (Jer 20.14–15):

> *Cursed be the day*
> *on which I was born!*
> *The day when my mother bore me,*
> *let it not be blessed!*
> *Cursed be the man*
> *who brought the news to my father, saying,*
> *"A child is born to you, a son,"*
> *making him very glad.*

We might think the New Testament would be sparse with curses, but there are plenty. Peter offers a curse when he denies that he is one of Jesus' followers (Mark

---

[24] See "A Curse-Prayer (Joshua 6.26)" in *Praying Through the Bible, Volume 1 (Genesis–Joshua)* (2015).

14.71);[25] Paul pronounces a strong curse on anyone who preaches a different gospel than the one he taught (Gal 1.9):

> *As we have said before, so now I repeat, if anyone proclaims to you a gospel contrary to what you received, let that one be accursed!*

As noted, blessings and curses often appear together, in a formula style: "if *this* then a blessing, if *that* then a curse." Noah blesses two of his sons but pronounces a curse on the third because of his shameful actions against his father (Gen 9.25–27).[26] Jesus offers four blessings and then contrasts it with four curses or "woes" (Luke 6:20–26). The book of Revelation contains many blessings and curses—a whole series of them appear in Revelation 22.7–18.

These examples of prayer-blessings and prayer-curses show us that they can enrich our prayer lives. It is likely that most of us do not think too deeply about blessings, only offering them before meals, weddings, and other particular occasions. Yet blessings can play a more significant role in our lives. Curses are more difficult—many of us might think that God would not want us to curse anyone. Curses can be misused: Rebekah places a curse on herself to help her son deceive his father (Gen

---

[25] He does it twice in Matthew 26.72, 74.

[26] See "Noah's Blessings and Curses (Gen 9.25-27)" in *Praying Through the Bible, Volume 1 (Genesis–Joshua)* (2015).

27.12–13);[27] Abner pronounced a self-serving curse (2 Sam 3.9).

In the New Testament, Paul wrote: "bless and do not curse" (Rom 12.14). But he is writing to those who are persecuting his readers. How can curses be used correctly in modern Christian life?

The best way is to learn about them in context—perhaps more so than any other prayer type. Every volume of *Praying Through the Bible* contains some, and you can decide for yourself the most responsible way to use them.

While blessing-prayers may be familiar to us (especially over meals), curse-prayers may be unknown. But both are often found in scripture, and blessing-prayers are liberally offered throughout. Curse-prayers are more rare, and perhaps the one type that we should take great care and study before offering—if ever.

---

[27] See "A Blessing Wrought in Deception (Gen 27.7, 12–13, 27–29; 28.2-4)" in *Praying Through the Bible, Volume 1 (Genesis–Joshua)* (2015).

Studying the Bible

Studying the *prayers* of the Bible uses the same approach as studying any *passage* of scripture. How do we go about these studies? Can we not just read the text and find the meaning is clear? Yes. But the characteristics of the Bible means that further study is needed if you want to go deeper in your knowledge.

The Bible was written thousands of years ago, over a period of about 1,200 years, in a culture that was not like ours. That gap sometimes means that we need to explore the ancient context to avoid misunderstandings. While we might wish that "God's Word" would not need such study, God revealed his Word through people writing in their own language in the own culture. (A caveat: I believe the subjects that are necessary to be a genuine follower of God require little, if any, study. The issues of salvation, imitating God in word and deed, and so on, are clear.)

But to go deeper, we need to do some work. God chose to direct his Word through humans and also chose to have these documents *preserved* by humans. The Bible did not drop down from heaven with its words divorced from a particular time, culture, or historical setting. If God had chosen to make everything easy for a 21st century Christian to understand, then an ancient person would have found much of it baffling. It is easier for a modern person to figure out how ancient people thought than the other way around. So God, in His infinite wisdom, chose for to preserve the Bible through the Ancient Near East and the Greco-Roman world, in Hebrew, Aramaic, and Greek, and with all the historical and cultural peculiarities that go along with those contexts. Sometimes we will have to do some digging to make sure we understand a passage.

There is more. It does not take a lot of detailed studies to realize that each book of the Bible has its own style and character. God did not quash the personalities and styles of the writers. He allowed them to write in their own way. This should not surprise us, for God has always worked through people, without making them into robots or dictation machines.

So, if we want to explore the meanings of these ancient texts, we need to bridge the gap between that world and ours. That means addressing history, culture, language, and society. This might not always be easy. Even today, people who travel from the Western world to the Middle East find themselves confused (and sometimes offended) by that culture (the reverse is true, too). The Bible portrays a Middle Eastern culture two or three thousand years ago; that span of time adds even more differences. The good news is that many researchers have spent centuries studying those cultures, and their work is easily available. In this book, it is my task to sort through that research, and note the most important elements when it will help is understand prayer better.

Once we have placed a passage in its context as best we can, the next step is to ask if the passage about prayer (or anything else) is a *practice* that God commands, or a *principle* couched in ancient cultural language? Let's look at some passages to explore this question. In some New Testament passages, women are urged to keep silent in public gatherings (e.g., 1 Tim 2), while other passages depict women speaking freely in public worship (e.g., 1 Cor 11). Some use this as a way to dismiss the Bible, saying it contradicts itself, but that is a naïve view of culture, history, and life itself. Just like in today's world, there were subcultures in every part of that world. Just like today, there were different situations and contexts even within a single subculture.

So one way of interpreting these passages is this: there were places in the Roman Empire where it was considered inappropriate for women to speak in public; there were others where it was acceptable in some situations. So one interpretation of those passages is that each reflects a different subculture, and not a particular practice we must follow. Instead of a command (which would contradict each other), we see a *principle* to follow: "people ought to act appropriately in public assemblies." In other words, what one should or should not do sometimes depends on the circumstances.

Others, however, see these passages as commands, though still related to their differing contexts. Timothy was writing a command: God does not want women speaking in public. Paul (in 1 Corinthians) was addressing a different issue, which was a principle: worship services should be orderly (and they were rather chaotic in Corinth).

These are two examples of trying to determine context and then meaning. It is up to you to decide which one seems the more likely. But without studying that's culture, one is left with either "the Bible contradicts itself" or "Paul (or Timothy) was wrong. Neither of those is useful, and make no sense if we think the Bible is God's word. The best option is a careful study of the context of a passage, along with some humility and an awareness that we may not have all the answers.

Let's look at another example that might be less controversial. It was the practice of the earliest Christians to meet in homes, and the New Testament implies that this is what Christians should do. Is this a practice commanded by God: "Christians should meet (only) in homes"? If so, most of Christendom has violated the word of God for many centuries. But perhaps it is only a principle: "Christians should meet regularly." *Where* they met was a matter of culture, history, and necessity.

The above leads us to realize that we must also critique ourselves. We might not like to admit it, but we have our biases and blind spots. For example, we are usually tempted to argue that something we practice as a command is correct, and anything we only see as a principle can be applied in different ways. But this is merely a way of saying, "what I have been doing is correct—what I already think is a command is a command; what I already think is a principle is a principle." In other words, "what I already do is correct, and anything other view is wrong." But this implies that we should never question existing practice and tradition, and that God has nothing new to teach us. (If we have that attitude, He probably can't!)

What if what we "think is obvious" is incorrect? Look at 1 Peter 1.3–4, which commands women not to braid their hair or wear jewelry. Most of us would say that the command was cultural—a principle that women (or anyone?) should take care how they dress in worship. Yet could we be guilty of imposing our culture on Scripture? It is a difficult question. Sometimes, studies that contextualize can help. For example, there is a good reason to think the passage was initially addressing a particular situation. In some areas of the Roman Empire, prostitutes braided their hair and wore it loose, while married women wore their hair bound up. Some Christian women, especially Greek women, may have thought that "being free in Christ" meant being free of social restraints. Perhaps the writer of the letter wanted to ensure that Christian women did not show up at worship services looking like immoral women. Another option is this: since the Roman Empire drew strict divisions between classes and status, perhaps the writer did not think worship was a place to divide by class (which would be obvious by the clothing and adornment worn). With these two pieces of information about the Roman Empire, we can conclude (without choosing between them) that the issue was larger than just what women wore—there is a principle to uphold rather than a specific practice to follow.

It is not always so simple, of course, and sometimes we do not know enough to make complete sense of a passage. However, such ambiguous passages are rare, and they rarely impact a core theological or doctrinal practice. (It is also important to note that our salvation does not depend on the proper interpretation of every practice. God offers grace—not only for our sins but also for our honest misunderstandings about church practice.)

When we study the prayers of the Bible, the same questions arise about context, commands, and principles. Asking those questions and analyzing the contexts tells us a lot about how to understand a prayer.

This book, and the *Praying Through the Bible* series, uses a three-part method of study and interpretation. While not able to answer all questions, this approach usually reveals issues that help us understand their passage better. In the next chapter, I'll explain this three-part method and show examples of how it works.

A Three-Part Method for Studying the New Testament

Our goal is a lofty one: to learn as much as we can about the prayers in the Bible, their contexts, background, language, place in history, and literary forms. Then we want to apply its meaning to our own, modern prayers.

How do we go about such a task? The best way is using a standard three-part method. Its goal is twofold. First, to attempt to understand a passage/chapter/book in its original context. That is, how would the writer and the first readers have understood it? Our second goal is to apply the meaning in the original context to our own situation; that is, to understand it in modern terms.

Studying the Bible can sometimes get complicated, because, as we noted earlier, it was not just handed down from heaven like a set of laws. It grew out of real-life situations which were recorded, preserved, and edited by Jews and Christians in later times and cultures.

For example, let's look at Paul first letter to the church in Corinthian. While modern believers see this as "a book in the Bible," with chapters and verses, the original readers did not. For them, it was an actual letter, written in the style of ancient letters (though much, much longer than most), by a Christian leader, to a congregation of believers who lived in the city of Corinth in Greece. Paul wrote it to a congregation that he had worked with for eighteen months, who were having some arguments about their Christian practices and beliefs. It was not part of a "Bible." It had no chapters or verses. We can call this context **Level One**: the original context. A Jewish man, now a leader of a new sect of Judaism, wrote a letter to a congregation made up of Jews and Gentiles, who lived in the large and cosmopolitan city in Greece. He wrote it in Greek. What would the passages have meant to them in their context? And how do we try to get inside their context?

Now, I pick up my Bible and turn to First Corinthians and begin reading. The "book" I read has been given a title, chapter, and verse divisions, and perhaps even cross-references and footnotes. I am reading an English translation. I am a product of the United States in the early 21st century. I grew up in a particular Christian tradition, one of many traditions that have evolved over the last 2,000 years. It doesn't seem like any letter that a modern person would write, and it doesn't read like one. For me, it's the Word of God. How will I understand those words? And how can I make sure I don't impose my experience and context onto it? This is **Level Two**.

In some passages and books, there could even be another level. This would be in passages that record a story or event. For example, consider a story about the prophet Samuel in First or Second Samuel. While we still have Level One (the original writer and readers) and Level Two (you and I), there is another level that might not be apparent at first. It is the context and meaning of their events *as they took place*. After all, there was not a writer standing there, recording everything that Samuel did and said. Someone wrote all that down later. If you could go back in time and watch the event happen, that's another level. Later, someone wrote it story down, which is a different level (what we called Level One above).

We could even add a fourth level for books that were edited later—this would be a lot of the books of the Old Testament, when the religious leaders in exile edited them.

It's a lot to think about, but it can open up so much more of God's word. Just reading the Bible, with no thought or knowledge or exploration, cannot lead us to deeper understanding. If we do that, we are only reading at level two. Georg Christoph Lichtenberg, a German scientist and satirist, said it this way:

A book is a mirror. If a monkey peers into it, surely an apostle can't look back out.[28]

Just reading a book as full of meaning as the Bible is not enough for a deep understanding. That would merely be reading ourselves into it. There are too many differences in time, culture, geography, language, and world-view. This is true of anything you might read that is outside your context. That is why, if you want to gain

---

[28] Georg Christoph Lichtenberg (1742-1799). (Ein Buch ist ein Spiegel, wenn ein Affe hineinguckt, so kann freilich kein Apostel heraus sehen.)

a solid understand Homer's *Odyssey*, Aristotle's *Ethics*, or Shakespeare's plays, you have to study them and their context and literary structure.

At this point, you might say, "But, Dr. Markus, this is the Bible we are talking about. It is more than *just* ancient literature, isn't it? Is it right to use the same methods?" Excellent question, and it is true that the Bible is not the same as an ancient piece of literature because it is "inspired" (whatever you think that word means). The difference lies in the meaning and in the way God worked through the writers, editors, and preservers of the texts. Yet it *is* still ancient literature. Like Shakespeare, it was written in a specific language, in a particular time, from a certain world-view. To explore those contexts is to take it seriously, even if the *meaning* is eternal.

But another reader might pipe up and say, "So we all must get degrees in ancient studies, literature, and history before we can understand the Bible? Easy for you to say!" Another excellent point, and my answer is "absolutely not." The Word of God is clear enough in its essential message. If you just want to read the Bible, and never give a thought to context, history, language, and literature, you can still be a faithful servant of God. It is not *understanding* the Bible that makes us faithful followers, it is our dedication to Him and His ways and living as he intends. Of course, one would still have to have a basic understanding of God as creator and sustainer, His character, the nature of sin and its consequences, God's remedies for it, the nature of who Jesus is and the meaning of the Cross, and the role of the church. Think of the Apostles Creed: if one could read it and live it, without ever reading a Bible, they could be a faithful follower of God. Their faith would be missing a lot of richness, but they would believe and live the basics.

But if you are a believer who wants to go deeper in your understanding, or wants to understand what the fuss is all about, this three-part method will help. We'll apply this as we study the prayers of the Bible. The process begins by looking **Behind the Text**, that is, exploring any history, culture, language, and so on that will help us understand the original context of the prayer. Next, we explore **In the Text,** where we examine the words themselves as literature: structure, literary devices, original language techniques (like a play on words or a pun), etc. This helps us in understanding the meaning of the prayer from inside it. Finally, we go **In Front of the Text**, which helps us consider our own context. We do this for two reasons. First, to try to avoid imposing our culture or context on the Bible, and second, to find a way to apply it to a modern Christian (the relevant application).

Putting all three of these together can give us a reasonably solid understanding of all aspects of each prayer. In the next three chapters, we'll consider at each in turn.

"Behind" the Text

Introduction

In the last chapter, we looked at the three "worlds" that every prayer lives in (indeed, every passage of scripture). In this chapter, we'll explore the first one and how to apply it.

Behind the Text

This approach is an "author-centered" approach. That is, we are trying to find out as much as we can about the author's context. We don't need to know who the author is, though that might give us some clues to the context. We want to examine the language, social world, history, culture, and so on. The more we know, the better we can read and understand the prayer.

Many years ago I was walking along a cliff above a beach, and I found a letter among some boulders. I pulled it out from a crevice and scanned the seven or eight pages. The writer was upset with someone—maybe more than one person, it was not clear. The author mentioned some specifics, but it was mostly reactions and thoughts based on an event or events that the author and recipient both knew. Based on what was said, I could make some guesses about the people, the relationships, and the events. But without more context,

I could not fully understand it. Of course, I could have merely interpreted the letter based on my own reactions to the words and my own life experience. But I might be missing some crucial information of context that would utterly change my understanding. What if this was a teenager? A grandmother? What if it was not left there by the recipient, but by the author who decided not to send it? What if it was a fiction, made up by someone who was writing a story? Or an attempt to write someone else's story? Or a school project to write a letter that a character in a film might have written?

With biblical texts, it can be even more difficult than something written in my own time, language, and culture. In the prayers of the Bible, an ancient writer was writing in another a language, culture, and time different than mine (let's call this the "cultural filter"). As I read the prayer, I am doing so through my language, culture, and time (this would be my "cultural filter"). To do a better job of understanding these filters, I need to take both of into account. Exploring "behind the text" deals with the first filter: the one that belongs to the author. The primary elements of this filter are language, culture, and history.

Language

Let's examine the "language" distance by looking at the following passage from the first mention of prayer in the Bible:

"Behind" the Text

> *At that time people began to invoke the name of the LORD. (Gen 4.26)*

When you read the word "Lord" what comes to mind? A synonym for God? If so, what image? Or perhaps you think of Jesus, who is often called "Lord" in the New Testament, but then realize that this must be God in this passage. Maybe you think of it as a title for God, like one might address a king of a country or a judge of a court in the United Kingdom.

There are many words in Hebrew that are translated as "Lord" into English. A common one is *adonai*, which means "lord," "sir," or "master." It is used to address persons in authority, but it is also used as a formal title for God. Another word, not as common, is *El* or *Elohim*, which is merely a general word to mean god—whether the God of Israel or pagan gods. Often, in the Bible, *el* is used with another word to make it into a title, such as *el shaddai* ("God Almighty") or *el elyon* ("God Most High").

The word used here is neither of those. Here, it is a translation of a Hebrew word rendered into English as *YHWH*, sometimes written as *Yahweh*. It is a strange word in Hebrew and is unpronounceable the way it has come down to us in the biblical texts. In Exodus 6.2, Moses experienced the presence of God through a burning bush. When Moses asked who He was, God tells him he is the one who appeared to Abraham, Isaac, and Jacob as *el shaddai*. Then he tells Moses that He only made himself known to them in part, but now he would reveal his true name to Moses: *YHWH*.

The word is probably a form of the Hebrew verb "to be" (which is why some Bibles translate it "I Am") A better translation, though more cumbersome, is "I will be what I will be." It is not a general word of description or a title. Instead, it is God's *actual name*.

The writer who wrote Genesis wanted to make it clear just who this God was: not some distant god, not some uncaring god, but the God *YHWH* himself, who had revealed himself to Moses at the burning bush.[29]

That would be the cultural filter of the people who read that passage for the first time. Quite different from ours! Knowing that information about language can help us read that passage better—the people living in Egypt, suffering in slavery, *know* who they are praying to, and that he loves them.

Social World

The social world, or culture, that existed when a prayer passage was written also gives us some important clues to its meaning. We should not really say "the culture of the Old Testament" or the "New Testament culture" because, like today, there were many subcultures. We might speak of "American culture," but there are other subcultures at play that might affect our understanding of something: New England culture, southern culture, or California culture, for example. Even in a smaller

---

[29] Over time, that name became so sacred that the Jews chose to never say it aloud. Instead, they substituted the word *adonai*, the phrase "The Name," or some other word or phrase.

area, such as England, we might need to distinguish between the London metropolitan area, Wales, or Cornwall.

Let's look at two mentions of prayer in Deuteronomy 26:

> *"I have removed the sacred portion from the house, and I have given it to the Levites, the resident aliens, the orphans, and the widows, in accordance with your entire commandment that you commanded me; I have neither transgressed nor forgotten any of your commandments: I have not eaten of it while in mourning; I have not removed any of it while I was unclean; and I have not offered any of it to the dead. I have obeyed the LORD my God, doing just as you commanded me.*
>
> *Look down from your holy habitation, from heaven, and bless your people Israel and the ground that you have given us, as you swore to our ancestors—a land flowing with milk and honey."*

There are a lot of phrases in this section that may make little sense to us: "sacred portion," "not eaten of it while mourning," "while unclean," and "offered any of it to the dead." If we do not do any background study (behind the text) we may be left to misread these test, or, more likely, just ignore it because it doesn't make sense.

How would an understanding of this prayer begin? First, we remind ourselves that the people who wrote and lived in these stories belonged to pre-industrial age —their culture was organized around agriculture, unlike ours. It is not surprising that many of the ceremonies, prayers, and religious instructions revolve around the agricultural year. Had the Bible been written in the 20th or 21st century, the prayers would have a different cycle and setting.

This passage concerns offering "first fruits" to God, that is, a portion of the first harvest of the year. After the bleakness of the winter, where the people ate mostly food they had stored and preserved from the previous year, the crops were planted and grew. When the first of the fruits and vegetables were ready, it was only right to dedicate some of the new, fresh produce to God.

Most of us have little experience in agrarian culture. We can buy almost any kind of produce all year around, only by visiting the grocery store or even having it delivered! But those ancient people worked hard to prepare the soil, plant seeds, tend the crops, and examine the first crop was ready to know how the rest of the harvesting season would unfold. From a seed comes food and drink that sustains life, provides meals for social occasions, and provides part of the economy of buying and selling that drove society.

The first harvest was the time to take some of that produce and give it to the priests for sacrifice, to the poor, and to orphans and widows as a way of thanking God for a new agricultural season. They sacrificed a bit of what they had, giving back to Him in thanksgiving and gratitude.

Most us in our day do not have this experience. But the example still applies, and in studying such prayers we ask how we could offer "first fruits" to God that does not involve agricultural products, but something from our own lives in this culture.

History

The history behind any prayer passage could also be a key to understanding it. For example, in 2 Chronicles 14.14-15, we read this:

> *They took an oath to the LORD with a loud voice, and with shouting, and with trumpets, and with horns. All Judah rejoiced over the oath; for they had sworn with all their heart and had sought him with their whole desire, and he was found by them, and the LORD gave them rest all around.*

With no background study, we might not even realize that the "oath" being taken here is actually a prayer-vow—a prayer that makes a promise to God. We might also wonder why all the excessive celebration? But the historical context of this passage opens it up for us. King Asa became the ruler the southern kingdom (Judah) of Israel. His father, Abijah, and been a terrible king who worshipped other gods and brought many pagan practices to Israel. But his son carried out religious reforms when he took the throne. God sent the prophet Azariah to tell Asa that God was with him, and that Judah had been unfaithful for a long time and had been punished for it. But now that Asa was returning Judah to faithfulness, God would bless him and the people. This renewed Asa's desire, and he had all the idols from the land removed, repaired the altar at the Temple, and then gathered all the people together for a covenant renewal ceremony. The prayer above was offered after many sacrifices; the nation pledged themselves to God and offered a vow (oath) that they would devote themselves utterly to God. With an understanding of the history, the power of renewal and rededication explains the profound meaning of this prayer, just like a prayer we might offer after we have been unfaithful for a long time.

Other, crucial events in history lie behind a lot of the words of prayers in the Bible. The delivery from Egypt, led by Moses, and the destruction of Jerusalem and the exile of the people to Babylon were the two most crucial events in the history of the Jews. Many later passages and prayer refer back to those events. The Gospel of Matthew even presents Jesus as a "New Moses" who gives commands from a mount and will lead his people to a new promised land.

Another crucial event of the period was the destruction of the Jewish Temple by the Roman army in 70 AD (the "second" Temple which had been rebuilt by King Herod). Some New Testament documents were written before that event; some were written after. In Mark, Jesus foretells the destruction of the Temple. Some later letters refer to it symbolically. Knowing as much as we can about that event, its precursors, and the aftermath, can help us dig deeper into the meaning and purpose of the passages and books we study.

Conclusion

Going "behind the text" allows us to dig deeper into a passage or a book. While the primary message of any prayer might be clear, by exploring its context, we can uncover further details and insights we might otherwise miss. Together with the other two methods, this approach goes a long way toward helping us enrich our prayers.

"In" the Text

This chapter addresses the second method of prayer study called "In the Text." This approach is "text-centered" rather than "author-centered." That is, we are not looking at the circumstances behind the writing of the prayer, but instead, we are examining the text of the passage itself. This means asking questions about genre, structure, and looking for literary elements. If you remember anything from your old English Lit classes, it will now come in handy.

literary analysis is a complex and broad area of study, but the following gives you an idea of how it works.

Consider a short story. There was an actual person who wrote it, who lived in an actual world, and who was writing for a particular reader or readers. Yet there is also a world that exists in the story itself. There is an author or narrator, who may be different from the "real" author. Think about a movie or a book with a narrator. The person who wrote the screenplay or book is probably different from the fictional person who narrates it.

The world of the story can also be entirely different from the real world of the author. Again, think of a movie or a book that takes place in the future, or in a fantasy land. But even if it takes place in the "real" world, it has its own character.

There may also be an implied reader who is not the same as the real reader. For example, consider the classic novel *Moby Dick* by Herman Melville. While

Melville is the "real" author, the story purports to be told by Ishmael, a sailor writing about the captain of a whaling ship. The world in the story is quite similar to Melville's world, but not exactly—the boat, fisherman, and others items did not really exist in his world. Melville created a *story world* based on his real world (and on sailing legends about a monstrous whale). On the other hand, Tolkien's *The Lord of the Rings* takes place in the world created entirely by the "real" author. In both of those books, there does not appear to be any implied reader. But consider a nonfiction book, *The Screwtape Letters,* written by Tolkien's friend, C.S. Lewis. The book is purportedly a series of letters from a chief demon to a novice demon, explaining how to turn humans away from God. The purported reader (the "narratee") is the novice demon, but the "real reader" is a person, like you or I, who picks up the book.

Genre

Before we study any biblical prayer, we should determine the genre of the book in which it is found. When we receive a letter, we unconsciously read it differently depending on its "genre." If the letter is from the electric company demanding payment, I read it differently than I would if it were a letter from a long-lost friend. You read a love letter with different suppositions than a legal letter (hopefully). We do not read poems the same way we read a newspaper article.

"In" the Text

It should be no different when we read a prayer in a book of the Bible. Regarding overall genres, the Bible contains **narratives** (parts of Exodus, Ruth, Acts); **poetry** (Psalms, almost all of Job, some prayers in the New Testament letters, parts of Revelation); and **regulations or law** (parts of Deuteronomy and Numbers).

But there are other genres and subgenres as well. Here are a few:

1. **Wisdom Literature** (Proverbs, Job, Ecclesiastes), which asks questions or makes statements about the meaning and purpose of life, either practically or philosophically.

2. **Prophetic literature** Words of God's representatives to His people guiding them or warning them (Isaiah, Jeremiah, Hosea, Amos, etc.)

3. **Gospels** (Matthew, Mark, Luke, John) these are narratives, but are not purely a biographical or historical narrative—the material is arranged and told in a way to emphasize the *meaning* of Jesus' life more than a chronology of events.

4. **Ancient Letter.** (some sections of Kings and Chronicles, the 21 letters in the New Testament, parts of Revelation). Though they do not look like letters we would write, they are written in the way ancient people wrote letters.

5. **Apocalyptic Literature.** (Daniel, part of Mark 13 and 2 Thessalonians, Revelation). This is a unique and distinctive type of writing, all written over

about a 400-year period in times of great suffering and distress for Jews and Christians. These writings were meant to give a "big picture" view of the world and its events, to encourage those who were suffering to know that God was in control (even if it didn't seem like it).

Literary Elements

The prayers embedded in these various genres often are connected to the genre in their purpose, meaning, and sometimes even structure and their own genre. Prayers can include a narrative, such as this section from the lengthy praise and thanksgiving prayer in Judges 5.21-31):

> *"LORD, when you went out from Seir,*
> *when you marched from the region of Edom,*
> *the earth trembled,*
> *and the heavens poured,*
> *the clouds indeed poured water.*
> *The mountains quaked before the LORD, the One of Sinai,*
> *before the LORD, the God of Israel.*

Many prayers contain poetry, of course, especially those of the Psalms, or this praise-prayer of victory after God delivered the Israelites from the Egyptian army from Exodus 15:

> *"I will sing to the LORD, for he has triumphed*

> *gloriously;*
> *horse and rider he has thrown into the sea.*
> *The LORD is my strength and my might,*
> *and he has become my salvation;*
> *this is my God, and I will praise him,*
> *my father's God, and I will exalt him.*
> *The LORD is a warrior;*
> *the LORD is his name.*

Literary analysis of the passages in which prayers occur asks *why* is it written *this way?* By exploring that question, we take the Bible seriously and gain more profound insights into its intended meaning. Those who wrote down the words of the Bible employed these genres and other literary techniques, just as we all do when writing (even if we do not realize that we are doing so).

There are many more subgenres and techniques than described below, but this list will give you an idea of how literary analysts if prayer works and what to look for.

Metaphors. The Bible is filled with metaphorical language. A metaphor is a rhetorical device where a writer or speaker uses an unrelated idea or thing to explain the meaning of something else. It is used because the unrelated thing has some characteristics that are the same as the main subject. Light and darkness are often used in the Bible as a way of understanding spiritual insight or salvation, whereas "darkness" usually refers to spiritual blindness, sinfulness, or being cut off. Note the use of darkness in this prayer from 1 Samuel 2 (Hannah's praise-prayer):

He will guard the feet of his faithful ones,
  but the wicked shall be cut off in darkness;
  for not by might does one prevail.

On a more positive note, here is a call to prayer from Revelation 19.7:

Let us rejoice and be glad and give the glory to
Him, for the marriage of the Lamb has come
and His bride has made herself ready.

There are three metaphors in this verse: lamb, bride, and marriage. Jesus is not *actually* a lamb, but the metaphor means that he is a sacrifice for sin and deliverance, like the lamb of the Passover celebration. The church is not a real bride, but as the partner of the groom (Jesus) who will nurture, care for, and protect the church. Finally, the marriage is a metaphor for the union of the church and Jesus in heaven at the end of time.

Symbols. A literary symbol is similar to a metaphor, so much so that many use them interchangeably. But in strict terms, a symbol is not used rhetorically, but is a specific thing that directly represents another thing (a metaphor is a more complex way of presenting one thing as another). A symbol often cuts across time and setting, and is used by larger groups of writers or speakers, unlike a strict metaphor, which is usually "invented" by a writer or speaker (see above). For example, the term "sheep" is often used as a symbol for the followers of God. Sheep gather and move in herds, and are dependent upon a herder to care for and direct them.

This became a natural symbol for devoted followers. So, Jesus is the "Good Shepherd," and the church is the flock of sheep who hear his voice, recognize him, and follow him (Matthew 9:36; 10:6; 26:31; John 10:11, 16, 26.)

An excellent example is found in a series of prayers from 2 Kings 6. In the first, vv17-18, Elisha's servant is afraid because they are surrounded by enemies. Elijah prays:

> *"O LORD, please open his eyes that he may see."*

The servant then becomes aware that a vast army of God stands behind and around the enemies. So, while he "sees" them physically, it is also a symbol of spiritual insight—he had to see physically before he was able to "see" spiritually, whereas Elisha already believed God was with them. Elijah prays again:

> *"Strike this people, please, with blindness."*

The enemies are blinded (literally, but also spiritually, because they are fighting against God. Elisha takes them to the capital city to be put under guard. Once there, he prays once more:

> *"O LORD, open the eyes of these men so that they may see."*

After the prayer, the soldiers can see physically, but more importantly, they have "seen" the power of God. "Sight" is being used as a symbol in the story.

Parallelism. Another type of analyses looks at the structure of prayer. One such technique is that of parallelism. This is common in ancient writings, especially in Hebrew literature, but is also found in Greek manuscripts. This is where one line parallels a second, either in subject, thought, structure, or content. Often this is how poetry is written in the Bible. For example, Mark 11.9-10 reads:

> *Blessed is he who comes in the name of the Lord! Blessed is the kingdom of our father David!*

Each begins with the same word, then describes what it is that is blessed. Parallelism is used to emphasize an idea, word, or phrase, but it also made it easier to learn in a culture where books and writings were not readily available.

It is not only poetic prayers that include parallelism—other genres do as well. Note the complex parallelism of words and similar ideas in the prayer-hymn in the letter of Philippians (2.9-11):

> *Therefore God also **highly exalted him** and gave him the name that is **above every name**, so that at the name of Jesus **every knee** should bend, in heaven and on earth and under the earth, and **every tongue** should confess that Jesus Christ is Lord, to the glory of God the Father.*

Conclusion

Going "in the text" allows us to dig deeper into a passage or a book by treating it for what it is: literature. Taking God's word seriously, we can ask about its genre, subgenera, and what we might learn by looking for literary devices and structure. Together with the other two methods, this approach goes a long way to helping us enrich our own prayers.

"In Front" of the Text

If the first method ("behind the text") was author-centered, and the second ("in the text") was text-centered, then this method is "reader-centered." Yes, you and I are the focus of this method!

How can a reader be a subject of study for understanding biblical prayers? Because, just like the author and the text itself, each of us, as we read, has a "setting"—a context. And as we read, we become part of the process of hearing what those prayers have to teach us.

The Difficulty of this Method

This is the most difficult of the three-part method because it requires self-critique. What presuppositions do I hold about the Bible, the world, prayer, and God? What conscious and unconscious biases do I bring with me when I read? We may not like to admit we have biases—but everyone does.

Most of us, when we read the Bible, want to find that it supports everything we already believe. That's natural. Or perhaps we have a beloved parent or grandparent who believed certain things, and we will not want to discover that they were wrong. If our religious tradition is Catholic, or Baptist, or Anglican, we will tend to interpret the Bible to support the teachings of those traditions, even though we know that others might understand some parts differently.

More unconscious are the biases that have to do with our life experience and personality. The following are generalizations but can serve to illustrate the point. Someone who is politically liberal might tend to read the words of Jesus' as supporting their politics—so they emphasize support of the poor, acceptance, and forgiveness, and then apply the Bible to the role of government. That same person might downplay passages about responsibility, discipline, judgment, using passages that decry judgmentalisme. They also might deny any gulf between the Christian mission and the State's purpose. A political conservative would, accordingly, emphasize the latter and downplay the former. Someone who had terrible father figures in their life might read the passages about "God as Father" quite differently than someone who had excellent father figures. Someone who grew up in poverty might read passages about God blessing people with wealth and the church's responsibility to the poor differently than someone who grew up with great wealth.

But our human weakness and pride can lead us to deny these biases and perspectives. "Not me," we want to say. "I am aware of it all." Meanwhile, we criticize others who don't see that they are reading their upbringing, politics, or viewpoints into the prayers and the Bible.

Our environment, upbringing, personality, and worldview *will* affect the way we read the Bible—what we emphasize, what we dismiss, and even the way we interpret something. Whether or not we mean to, we impose meaning on what we read that it may or may not support.

It can be frustrating to encounter someone who reads the same passage quite differently than we do. Usually, we think it means they are wrong. But is it possible that *I* am wrong? And if so, how can I know? Does this leave us with a modern "it means whatever you think it means" method?

I do not think so. While a thorough critique of ourselves may not be possible, there are things we can do to be aware of our biases. The first step of this method is to admit that I have biases and perspectives, too.

We begin by recognizing that I might not always be right about a particular doctrine, belief, or practice. Once we can make peace with that possibility, we should seek out other views. They are easy to find: books, friends, internet articles, even your own congregation and family. Rather than immediately rejecting a differing viewpoint, try to understand *why* someone believes it. Ask questions, do research. Once you have some sense of it, try explaining that differing view to someone else.

If you always read, listen, and surround yourself with those who hold the same views, you lose any possibility of revelation and growth. We must be brave enough in faith to realize that we are likely wrong about *some* things.

An example prayer from Judges 17.1-3

The prayers in this passage, and the surrounding stories, are good examples to explore "in front of the text." Here are the two prayers:

> *"The eleven hundred pieces of silver that were taken from you, about which you uttered a curse, and even spoke it in my hearing..."*
> *"May my son be blessed by the LORD!"*
> *"I consecrate the silver to the LORD from my hand for my son, to make an idol of cast metal."*

The story is this: The prayers are offered by the mother of a man named Micah, who had stolen a good bit of money from his mother. When she discovered the theft (but not who had taken it), she asked for a curse to be placed on the thief. When Micah hears it, he is afraid, and he confesses and returns the money to her. His mother then asks God for a blessing on him.

A wayward son changes his ways, and his mother turns a prayer-curse into a blessing prayer. But then the mother takes some of the coins to a silversmith and has them melted down to make an idol. Micah makes a shrine for the idol and appoints his son as the priest. So, this is *not* a story about two faithful Israelites, but two wayward followers of God. Verse 6 tells us why the writer included the story: "In those days there was no king in Israel. Everyone did what was right in his own eyes."

In Front of the Text

Even with examining these prayers using the other two methods, we can apply this "in front of the text" method. Could we be as unfaithful as these two characters? Is there a way for us to become aware of unexamined attitudes and actions in our prayer and life that do not reflect God's ways? We, like those two, are embedded in our own culture. Some ideals of that culture will be in agreement with God's ways, but others will not. We should take the time to critique the values, expectations, and ideals of our culture and compare them with God's ideals. For example, modern American culture stresses individualism. You are your own person, and what you do is no one's business if it does not affect them. But self-centeredness runs counter to God's ways. The people of God are a community—we *do* have a responsibility towards others. Note the language used for believers: "body," "tribe," "family." Everything done by an individual in a family has some effect on the whole. If we adopted the cultural view, how might that negatively affect our prayers?

Likewise, our modern culture encourages us to be tolerant of all lifestyles and behaviors. At one level this is a sound idea. After all, Jesus interacted with tax collectors, gentiles, and prostitutes. But "tolerance" can become acceptance, which is not the same thing. Jesus had no problem condemning people—note his violent outburst when he drove the moneychangers and sellers from the Temple.[30] Befriending a prostitute and show-

---

[30] Mark 11:15–19, 11:27–33, Matthew 21:12–17, 21:23–27; Luke 19:45–48, 20:1–8); John 2:13–16.

ing that God loves everyone is spiritual work. *Accepting* a prostitute's actions and because it is her "choice" is not God's way. We are not called to condemn so much as to stand firm and to offer truth with grace, mercy, and love.

How does this apply to our prayers? Think about the character, attitude, and context of your prayers. How might your culture have influenced your time, manner, and attitude of prayer? How might it have influenced what you pray for? Can you spot any way that your prayers are influenced by your culture that is contrary to God's ways? Consider what you can do to change it.

Conclusion

Going "in front the text" alerts us to our part of the role in understanding the Bible and its prayers. While we can pray that God will guide us to understanding, our human weaknesses often lead us in ways we are not even aware of. This method allows us to practice some humility as we approach God's word, using all the tools He has given us, to enrich our own prayers.

An Example: Studying the Prayers of the Bible

We have learned the basics of the three approaches to studying prayer passages in the Bible (though it applies to any passage not just prayers). These methods give us some tools that impact how we read and understand the meaning of a passage—meanings we might not see if we had not done the background work.

To summarize: every prayer in the Bible falls into at least one of the nine categories of prayer we discussed at the beginning of this book. Knowing which one helps us to discern its purpose, and then help us use them.

The method "Behind the Text" provided us with insights into the historical context. The Bible contains stories that took place in the past: historical accounts, such as Judges, 1 Kings, Matthew, or Acts. Of course, they are doing more than *just* telling history, but that is the beginning point. Even if the story is not telling us history (Job, Psalms, the letters of the New Testament), the document was written and addressed issues at a particular time in history. So we ask: what historical events were going on around that time? What cultural values or perceptions—especially those different from ours—can help us understand a passage better? Taking this seriously is taking the Bible seriously.

An "In the Text" approach helps us to ask questions about the words, sentences, paragraphs, style, and structure. God saw fit to have a real person write these texts down, using their own language, context, and abilities. A study of the structure of a passage (or book), repetition, the choice of certain words, or their arrangement help us understand what God intended the writer to communicate. God chose *words* to convey his message to us—taking them seriously is taking his Word seriously.

Finally, the method we call "In Front of the Text" helps us realize our own part in understanding the Bible. God has created each of us as an individual, with our own personality, background, experiences, and expectations. For good or ill, all of that affects how we understand some passages. Being aware of these things about ourselves, and being able to analyze my *own context*, is a way to take God's creation (us) seriously as we seek to understand His message.

As you can see, doing this sort of background work is part of taking the Bible seriously. It gives us some boundaries and guidelines as we try to understand it. It helps to avoid making it "my word" instead of "God's Word."

Bringing The Three Methods of Bible Study Together

Not all three methods can be used in equal parts on every passage. Passages that tell us of a historical event can rely mostly on the first approach (behind the text). A poetic passage might depend almost exclusively on an approach that is literary (in the text). In most passages, though, the third will play a role (in front of the text). But all three usually have some role. Often, the three methods will interconnect, and the variation of amount and insight is almost as wide as the number of passages in the New Testament.

The best way to use the three methods is by choosing a text and applying it. This is what we will do when we turn to study the prayer passages. The following is an example—the prayer of Naomi in Ruth 1.8–9):

> *May the LORD deal kindly with you, as you have dealt with the dead and with me. The LORD grant that you may find rest, each of you in the house of her husband!*

Note how each of the sections below uses one or more of the three methods to explore the meaning of the prayer and how it can model prayer for us. The prayer is a petition, offered by Naomi upon her daughters-in-law upon the death of their husbands.

Background

The book of Ruth is the story of a mother and her daughter-in-law who show great love and devotion to each other. It is a story of losing and finding, humiliation and exaltation, despair and joy. The book has been the subject of many plays, literary works, and films—a testament to its message and its timelessness.

Teachers and pastors often cite Ruth as an example of devotion and perseverance. Yet those themes are not the primary reason why the story is part of the Bible. Some of the more troubling moral aspects of the characters' behavior are often swept under the rug in sermons and books.

Another aspect often overlooked relates to prayer. There are a *lot* of prayers in this short book (nine or ten, depending on how you define "prayer"). Why did the writer include so many more prayers per text than any other book? What does it teach us about prayer?

The story begins with a married couple living in a foreign land (outside of Israel). They have two sons who grow up and marry local women. The father dies, and ten years later, both sons die. The mother, Naomi, is now a widow in a foreign land with no family except two foreign daughters-in-law, who are also widows. This created a more serious problem than it would be today. With no male and no family, she has no one to provide for and protect her.

She decides to return to her homeland of Israel where she might find some long-lost relatives. She tells her daughters-in-law that they should remain in their own land, the land of *their* gods. They are young; they can find new husbands. Naomi is too old, and she does not expect the girls' new husbands to care for her—an old woman to whom they owe no obligation either by blood or law.

Naomi prays, asking God to deal kindly with the girls, just as He has dealt kindly in the past with Naomi, her husband, and their sons (1.8–9). She also asks that God help the women find husbands and security. It is likely that the girls' mothers and fathers are still alive.

They could return home in safety and with the possibility of remarriage. Naomi does not have those options.

Meaning

Naomi's prayer is noteworthy because the words seem to contradict the situation in which she finds herself. In ancient cultures, women were provided for by their father, husbands, sons, or surviving brothers. There was no welfare or retirement; there was no State aid. If a woman had none of those people in her life, she had few choices. The best she might do was to find work as a lowly servant in someone's household. Worse, she could sell herself into slavery or become a prostitute (this would not be an option for Naomi at her age). The only other possibility was to become a beggar. So Naomi's best hope was to return to her homeland of Israel, where some distant family members might be alive and could to take her in. If not, she would at least be among her own people.

Who would begrudge Naomi a prayer for God's protection? Who would criticize her for asking the two women to pray for *her*? Yet she does not pray for herself. Not only does Naomi ask God to help the two young women, she even hopes God will take care of them like He has taken care of Naomi and her family—all of whom are dead, leaving her in a foreign land alone.

What an impressive attitude in prayer! Naomi steps back from her trying circumstances—circumstances that could lead to starvation, abuse, and death—and focuses instead on God's past care. She notes how these young women have a whole life ahead of them and need to make secure decisions.

If we could speak to Naomi today and ask her why she prayed like this, I suspect she would say, "I lived a good and full life with a wonderful family. Tragedy has struck me, but that is the way of things. The next generation is what matters now, and I need to make sure my daughters-in-law are taken care of. It would be selfish and short-sighted of me to insist that someone comfort me to the disadvantage of the younger generation. I prayed as I should have."

Application

It is natural for our prayers to be self-centered. We often pray alone and in silence. What if, before we began our prayers, we considered our circumstances (good or bad) in light of the larger picture of our life? What if we could shift from seeing ourselves as the main character in the story, and instead see ourselves as one of many characters in a vast novel being written by God. How would that viewpoint change our prayers?

Write down specific intercessions or petitions you might usually offer in prayer this week. Look at that list, and imagine yourself as a great Director standing above your life and the lives of your family, your friends, and your community. Envision it as a complex story with many characters. The plot is the larger purpose of God. Does this perspective give you a different view of the requests you wrote above? How might you

An Example: Studying the Prayers of the Bible

remember to practice this exercise more often before you pray?

*

This is just one example, but it shows how the three methods open up new questions and new understandings. It is one of the ways to grow in our practice of prayer, and one that the Bible recommends: Paul says that believers should be able to "discern" the things of God—he uses a Greek word referring to study and analysis.[31] He tells the church in Thessalonica to "test" everything they believe and practice.[32] Timothy implies the same when he says that believers should be able to "rightly explain" their beliefs and practices. [33]

I hope you'll join me as we study prayer through the *Praying Through the Bible* series.

---

[31] Rom 12.12; 1 Cor 2.15
[32] 1 Thess 5.21.
[33] 2 Tim 2.15.

Resources

Books

- *Praying Through the Bible (Vol 1): Genesis-Joshua*
  - Amazon | Kindle | Apple Books
- *Praying Through the Bible (Vol 2): Judges-2 Samuel*
  - Amazon | Kindle | Apple Books
- *Praying Through the Bible (Vol 3): 1 Kings–2 Chronicles*
  - Amazon | Kindle | Apple Books
- *Praying Through the Bible (Vol 4): Ezra–Esther* (coming December 2018)

Online

- Praying Through the Bible project: http://www.prayingthruthebible.com
- Praying Through the Bible podcasts
  - Web: https://bit.ly/2l3lBZj
  - Apple podcasts: https://apple.co/2HIdfPX

- Spotify podcasts: https://spoti.fi/2Mn2qpU

Single Book Studies

- Genesis (Amazon | Kindle | Apple Books)
- Exodus (Kindle | Apple Books)
- Leviticus & Numbers (Kindle)
- Deuteronomy (Kindle | Apple Books)
- Joshua (Kindle| Apple Books)
- Judges (Kindle)
- Ruth (Kindle)
- First Samuel (Kindle)
- Second Samuel (Kindle)
- First Kings (Kindle | Apple Books)
- Second Kings (Kindle)
- First Chronicles (Kindle)
- Second Chronicles (Kindle)
- Ezra (Kindle | Apple Books)

Nehemiah and Esther coming in 2018.

A Note from the Author

With over a million books published a year, it means a lot that you are reading this one. Online reviews make a big difference, and if you can spare a few moments, please share your thoughts about the book at the online retailer where you purchased the book.

Just a few lines is enough to make a difference.
Thank you!

About the Author

Markus McDowell is an author & editor of fiction and nonfiction in multiple genres. He has a Ph.D. from Fuller Theological Seminary and a law degree from the University of London, and has lectured at universities in the US, Europe, and the UK. He is the author of the literary novel, *To and Fro Upon the Earth: A Novel*, and research works such as *Prayers of Jewish Women: Studies of Patterns of Prayer in the Second Temple Period*, *Prayer in the Ancient Stoic Tradition*, and the popular volumes on prayer, *Praying Through the Bible*.

If you enjoyed this book, please consider leaving an online review. The author would appreciate reading your thoughts.

Follow Sulis International Press

Subscribe to the newsletter: https://sulisinternational.com/subscribe/

Follow us:
https://www.facebook.com/SulisInternational
https://twitter.com/Sulis_Intl
https://www.pinterest.com/Sulis_Intl/
https://www.instagram.com/sulis_international/

www.ingramcontent.com/pod-product-compliance
Lightning Source LLC
Chambersburg PA
CBHW021444080526
44588CB00009B/684